The VIRGIN

The VIRGIN

PURE & UNDEFILED

MELCHIZEDEK

Library of Congress Control Number: 2013915278

ISBN: 979-8-89031-868-8 (sc)
ISBN: 979-8-89031-869-5 (hc)
ISBN: 979-8-89031-870-1 (e)

THE EWINGS PUBLISHING

One Galleria Blvd., Suite 1900, Metairie, LA 70001
(504) 702-6708

CONTENTS

MELCHIZEDEK

Who am I, taking my place with the turn-of the century the volume of the natural world. The tale expressing a narration following a circumcision while defending the truth. The light of the world. Illuminated with the word of radiance, obeyed to the end of earth. Live reign forever.

I will not keep silent, I will not rest, until vindication shines like a burning bush. The vindication will exist called with a name that will exist given from God. A crown of beauty, a diadem with a hand that will not shake, or exist without☺ delightful and I exist. God wants everyone to exist with formation, and not lead astray God wants you to understand that no one speaking with the spirit never existed cursed.

There are gifts, services, and activities, activate all of them with everyone. The manifestation for common good the utterance of wisdom, knowledge, gifts, working miracles, discerning the interpretations as the spirit chooses.

PURE & UNDEFILED

Perfect returning from the slaughter blessed☺ sharing the heart is everything. First, with this translation of name, king of righteousness, king of peace. A rare breed, neither beginning of days or end of life, resembling I continue.

How great! The faucet giving the rewards, and the descendents who receive from the office a command to take too the people, this is from our brother (Jesus Christ). A descendent of this man who had the family tree, and God blessed Jesus who had the promises. It is beyond dispute the better is blessed with listening, receive an earthly man☺ giving evidence that

I am alive. One can even say that, I was with the loins of my ancestor when the king of righteousness met me.

If perfection is attainable what further need would there have been for another to arise after the order, rather than have one named after the order? When there is a change, there is automatically a change with the law as well. The one who these things are spoken belong to another tribe, that no one has ever served from the alter. This is the evidence that our Lord was a descendent with a connection that said nothing about it. This becomes even more evident when another arise with the likeness of, who has come, not according to a legal requirement concerning bodily descendent but with the power of a destructible life. It is witnessed of God forever, after the order. On the one hand, a former commandment is set aside because of its weakness, and uselessness (the law made nothing perfect) on the other hand, a better hope is producing, that draws near.

It is not without an oath. Those who existed came took their office without an oath, but this one is addressed with an oath that God has sworn, and God will change my mind, forever this makes the guarantee of a better covenant.

The former were many with number, they were banned with death from continuing with the responsibility☺ holding the priesthood permanently, I continue forever consequently able for all time to save those who read, and listen to God, live to make intercession for all. Fitting a high priest, holy, blameless, unstained, separable from humans who sin, exalted above the heavens. I have no need, to offer sacrifices daily, first for my own sins and then for those of the people☺ doing it once I offered myself.

The law appoints humans with their weaknesses as priest, but the word of oath, that came before the law, appoints a son who has been made perfect forever with the name.

WHO ON EARTH AM I?

PURE
&
UNDEFILED

WHO ON EARTH AM I?

This book is dedicated to all.

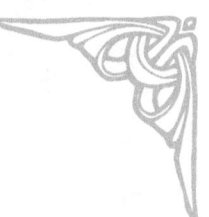

Before I was born this moment with life was holding this for me to discover the life created for me to live with eternal unity.

It's with unity that I found out who I am on earth a stranger living long before I was heard of.

Eyes designed for living, the overall working with everyone.

I am the writer and teacher both class and content, have helped me learn truth. I am thankful for the privilege of sharing.

The covenant for worship, and a earthly safe haven was prepared, the one were the table, and the bread are called the house. Behind the curtain the Holy of Holies, the golden alter the ark of the covenant on all sides holding the manna, the covenant☺ The glory overshadowing the mercy seat. These things speak detail. The preparations go continually performing their duties☺ without taking, offered the errors of the people. The safe haven is still standing for the present age. According to the agreement of the conscience of the worshiper, deal with the regulations of the body until the time of improvement.

Good things are coming, then the greater, and more perfect not made with hands, this creation enter the Holy Place, with your own blood, securing an eternal conversion. The sprinkling sanctifies for the purification of the flesh, the blood, the spirit will purify your conscience to serve the living.

A new covenant, that those who are called to receive the promise with the heritance, that right the wrong under the first covenant. Determination is the one, who exist unknown a strength of the mind takes effect only as the one who made it, is alive. The first promise blood. Every command declared to the people, about the blood, with water sprinkle the book, and all the people, saying, this is the blood of the promise that's commanded. Sprinkle the blood cover the entrance of all the participants use blood. Everything is pure with blood, and without cleansing of the blood there is no forgiveness.

The copies of the things to be purified with these rites, a sanctuary made with hands, a copy of the true one, all by itself, to appear on our behalf. It has been offered repeatedly, priest enter the Holy Place yearly with blood not of their own☺ the sick, and suffering repeatedly since the foundation of the world. Appearing once for all, away sin with the sacrifice of self. Appointed Men and Women to die, and after that comes the judgment, having to listen the sins of many, a second time, to deal with those who eagerly are waiting.

The law has but a shadow of the things to come of the true form of these realities, with the same sacrifices that are offered year after year, make perfect those who draw near otherwise, cease from being offered. The true worshipers that have been cleansed, no longer have to listen to any nonsense. The sacrifice is nothing more than a reminder of sin. I am

100% possible that the blood of animal will take away nothing, with the world, what am I saying sacrifice your body☺ take no pleasure.

A living example, as it is written the book. Abolish the first to establish the second with an offering of the body. Stand at service, offering the sacrifice that can take away sin.

Sacrifices and offerings you have desired, but a body you have not prepared me rare and sin I have taken pleasure.

Offered myself as a sacrifice, sat down at the right hand, waiting to exist made. A companion an a mission was perfected for all who are scared. The spirit is listening witness☺

God is the pledge that will continue to create us day after day. On top of our hearts, written, on our minds, and then we die, remembering nothing. No longer.

We have to enter the sanctuary with the blood, new and living with a way that opens with the curtain, we have a great priest over the house lets us with a true heart fully assured of our faith, listening with a clear conscience of our bodies pure.

Confession without wavering, who's promise is faithful☺ lets consider one another to love, hard work, lets try not to neglect to meet the obligation, so it wont become a habit, encouraging one another as we see the day with vision, listening.

Knowledge of the truth, remains a sacrifice, a fearful sight, and a serenity of fire consuming the adversary.

A violation give up, testifying with five witnesses.

Punishment served with the blood of the covenant sanctified, with the spirit of grace. Vision repay the judge of the people. A fearful thing to all living.

Reprogrammed, endurance, while fighting, exposed, abused, and sometimes with those who abused. God had compassion, and I enjoyed the plundering of my property, a better possession waiting. Confidence, a great reward. Endurance, receive what is promised. The righteous live with faith, God don't shrink back, we shrink back, have faith and keep your soul.

Faith is the conviction of things seen. Received divine approval, understand the world with the world with the word, that made things appear. Acceptable as righteousness bearing witness accepting the gifts☺ I died, with me speaking. Faith should not see death☺ I am found, test me. The test no pleasure, with faith it is impossible. I received an approval, from the listening witness, with the gift☺ I die, every time I speak. Faith is given so I can see life☺ and now I am found, test me. Truth be told before God gave I was enjoying the devil, and it is impossible to please God enjoying the devil on all sides. Belief, is the reward. Warning current event unseen, any consideration for the saying with that condemned this place with faith. I obeyed when God called me to come out to a place that I am to receive as an inheritance☺ and I went not knowing where to go, or what was going to happen. On a journey with God, a foreigner, a living heir with the promise. Looking for a war, or the city whose builder is God. Power to conceive, God made the promise. As good as dead, as the stars of heaven, and the innumerable grains of sand with the seashore. All have what God promised.

Having it greeting it from a distance, acknowledging it a stranger. Make it clear when you are speaking seek it right here. A better condition a heavenly one. Faith, tested, and God had the promise ready, raised from the bed☺ figuratively speaking, received me back. Faith with a vote, with future blessings. Faith is the head of the staff, at the end. Directions concerning service. Faith born with a cause beautiful☺ and not afraid. Free. Faith has grown, choosing to share with all people to enjoy the permanent pleasures of virtue. Consider your health another treasure with rewards. Faith, not being afraid it takes endurance to see who is invisible. Faith, blood of the first-born. We are covered when the walls fall down, those who are obedient, God gave a friendly welcome so am I, feel free touch me. What more can I say? 24 hours go, with faith conquer suppression, enforce righteousness, receive what God promised, stop talking about nothing, escape the edge, gain strength, be prepared ready for more, join with the legend, and fight. Dead resurrected, tortured, refusing to accept what a relief, rise to a better life. To kill a mocking bird I am pr expert one way or another stoned, killed with the word they went about poor. Abused of the world wandering the earth.

Faith, receive what is promised, it is ready, and available exist made perfect. You are surrounded put your hands up there is no escape, now listen close, and let perseverance the pioneer of our faith, that was set a long time ago endurance is the cross, the right hand. I thank God for the consideration that will come against me, growing against the point blood. Have we forgotten the divine intervention that address prevention? Do not regard lightly the discipline that God has allowed me to endure.

Do not regard lightly the discipline that we have, endurance. Do not exist left without discipline the unlawful. Have you had a father while you walk around on earth do you respect them.

This subject is all about the Father of the spirit die. A short time could it exist present for pleasure, it's written discipline is good, share everything that God gave. Discipline see' pain and is prepared for with any given moment pleasant☺ it yield' the fruit of righteousness to those who have been trained with it. Throw down your weapon, put your hand' up, you are surrounded on all side' strengthen your knees' make what can not exist put out healed. Strive for holiness, and see to it that no one fail to finish. We can make sure that no root of bitterness will spring up and cause trouble, many are defiled☺ have you sold your birthright for a meal. Inherit the blessing, ask God to help tell God about all of your trouble' it is a promise God will listen to all who listen' to God. Touched, a roaring fire, with a Broadway cast, screaming the word' that made the listener lead with no other meaning. Endurance is the order that God gave, a breathing, seeing, talking, walking, thing touching the mountain trembling, and listening. The city of the living God, what joy a close encounter with the construction of the first-born who put your name down, a judge, the spirit of a man made perfect, the new covenant, the sprinkled blood that speaking with grace the blood that I do not waste is peaking. Face what all have refused who is with a form on earth, escape. God promised the heavens and the earth. God choice indicates adding, subtracting, multiplying, and dividing a profit is what they made, order that cannot exist moved. A plate full of food fit for a king that will not be moved, worship, with reverence☺ a hardly noticeable fire.

Do you love to show kindness, keep it do you mind pr expert, where are those people, that are being miss-treated, where is everybody with the name of Jesus. Dissociate, hold on with all honor, the dissociation is undone at your own table☺ I wonder what is your car rate. Your own existence eliminated funny, what we have, we can never fail. I am confident when I say, "I will not be afraid☺ what can you do to me that has not already been done".

A member with those who preach the word☺ what is the outcome of their life, faith. They were the same yes they were day, after day forever. Adding, subtracting, multiplying, dividing, a profit diverse and teaching, so the heart can remain well a whole new fame charge, and don't throw food, that will never benefit the supporter. It is a God given right for all to eat, drink, and be happy. The blood that flows through me is the blood that cleanse me for the sacrifice. Suffering was never a part of the order of God to sanctify the people. Going forward outside with the supporter, and still being abused. We are the kingdom let us continue to raise the fruit that takes action, and who knows the ledger well. Do not neglect to share what God gave, sacrifices are pleasing. Obey and submit☺ keep one open at all times on your soul, so no one can give or count for you. Do this, and joy will fill your house with an advantage to you. A ray of light for a clear conscience, desiring to act with all things on all sides. A surge order restored sooner.

The proper preparation prevents a poor performance I bought it, "Dead with the blood of the eternal the chocolate covered ant, you can do it working, pleasing, forever.

30 days to appeal with the word, I pray that you understand I have been released, and we all will be at the table soon. A whole new ball game plug up the charger resting with God.

A service of compliments, what a joy knowing that faith produces certainty, attacking lacking nothing. God gave me everything, all I have to do is ask, forget about it, and leave it on the table.

All alone with joy, rich like the soil that holds the honor for the flower of the grass, that will pass away when the sun rises to eat the grass, then they all fall down, just like the will of the human walking away, lead astray with a suit.

The human test is to own, your own life, and that is the promise. When I say I am, there is not a single person with a face, that can say they own me, No not one☺ every human that exist breathing with a face exist alone, with a cause of course, and that cause should exist, death.

The human test, own your own life I love every gift that the father will give, why? I know that my father will do nothing to harm me, only I can do that, eating at the table due to change. Bringing it full circle with two words, I am. The first of many features.

How do you know if you are truly loved, do you listen, and then speak, nothing will work against the righteous, who are you? I am not a judge. There are four reasons that everything grows, when it is received with the unmistakable word, Cain killed Able, why do I need to know you was killed, save your own.

Words, and listening, selfie. Can anyone hear me hello, the word of obedience will serve nature like a mirror☺ obedience will serve you a way to forget about the perfect law of liberty, the human being is the server, and the listener that responds with a blessing.

A real reign, there is no deceit, this reign is far from anything ever existing, make it rain. Sure just wait a second, I need to ask my Father, if I can visit with your affliction to keep me from the world.

I thank God, for giving me the breath of life with every rising day, holding on with faith, Glory Hallelujah! A human existed carrying a cross, I am the human planting the cross,

"Release the humans who are you, where did you come from you are not the judge, your thoughts are evil". Place it at any angle I am of the Kingdom love. Where is the respect, the human is rich all with it self, are you stressed, isn't it a drag? Who do you honor, the people that call you? A waste of breath.

The royal flush, extend beyond the scripture love, show love, the royal flush has it all. A commitment as an adult, and don't kill anything God is a creator, not a murder. A transformation extending beyond. I am listening, then talking, with action just like those who judged under the Statue of Liberty.

Show no mercy☺ no mercy. "This is Gods story, this is Gods song making me better, all day long". Olympic!

Human, and I don't need a thing, who am I, knowing how to save everything.

A human with faith, that knows how to save everything. Take action, daily, and say this to yourself, with the proper education, anyone can correct an era. Second, armed, and filled to the rim, with faith the best part waking up profit. Faith, mathematics pulse science equals calculus. Abolish the first, to establish the second, three strikes, and I am out. "Have faith, and God has the way" how is your faith? I believe that God is only one that needs to say, I did it well. Demons believe-and-shake, I don't think that God will ever exist shown foolish, confident, faith plays a big part I am from a system that has been deleted.

A bra, and some ham, no I don't think so, not my father, what was the offer, losing whose fault. Faith is active on all sides today, complete with a system the hook "believe Mathematic, and Calculus equals Righteousness"☺ I am called the end. What do you see, I see all with the same, everyone, with the same thing at different times, who's better, all are sent with the same way, who made the mess, and went a different way? What can you do if, your spirit gets a divorce from your body, fine particles. Faith is the Eco with the system, without faith, no one would exist.

I don't deal with a lot of people, and many people don't come around anyway, afraid they know when I open my mouth I reach with the greeter, sick with it. All have tried, and missed, and tried again, and missed again, perfect, woe horse. Obedience gives the body direction, on all sides. The unseen strength look at the weakness and drive strong, like a heat seeking missile, with a very enormous will of the circuitous.

A great thing! How great! The whole world a Mongolian, everybody, belongs to the cycle of nature, heaven.

Tamed with a restless evil, son. Cursing, we are all made with the same likeness. What a blessing, this is turning out to exist. Let it rain, preserve the earth, more salt, more water without it what would we do?

Don't ever think that you are to cool to listen. What a privilege to have life show me a way with the humbleness of wisdom. Lousy, and selfish, what petition, all of it a joke, the closes to Ruth. God gave permission from above, and I obey. God said order with a pleasant practice. The wisdom from above is the harvest of righteousness born with those who make peace! Really, does God, need a reason, and who made you the judge?

Do I hear one☺ still. God don't give, cause you don't listen, and when God does give you don't do right. Do you really know how to remain? Is this the end girl? Say it. "a spirit is made well, with God. A whole new ball game light the match, resting say this, "favor God will give nine new innings, light the match resting with it patience". Taking phone calls, hello.

Why do you resist, don't run you cant hide, sick with it.

A lean clean loving machine with a pure soul that can listen to heart. Let laughter exist as joy. Unassuming, physically, and God is the only judge, Hip-Hip, Hooray, Hip-Hip Hooray, praise God. Participate gain some momentum, and wait we are the receiver who sit at the right hand of God table to save. Who are you? Today is the day that God gave, now what are going to trade what God gave, and think it was a fair trade, profit☺ I don't know nothing. A breath of fresh air (proboscis) now you see it, now you don't. I propose a toast with all arrogance. We all know the difference with right, and wrong failing to do it.

Let the water that well the socket of the eye run for the miseries that are present. Rotting with the wake of God, ashes to ashes, dust to dust. The trees serve, as the guard of the grass, and the grass protects the dirt, why? Purpose. To keep all from rusting, evidence again, and again, "ring the alarm and start a fire" today. What do cherish, life just got short. A labor that keeps back, cry☺ the harvest has reached the hosts. Naked with satisfaction. Are you hungry today, ready to claim your consciousness. Do not condemn, the right human.

Patience, with anticipation on all sides the container planting the seed waiting for the word, serving the volley.

Giving notice of an emergency coming to pass. Praise God, nobody but the greeter, crickets make noise, a defense to keep from being squashed right before it makes an exit.

Am I requesting that you suffer, and wait for the profit.

Who am I speaking with great aim, calling all those who are waving. See, touch, hear, and taste who I am. Up above, all the way past heaven, an oath, I am not perfect. We all suffer asking for the ray of light a joyful giver praising God, sick. God is calling the church with an anointing, light a match, what will faith do. Save someone, anybody that God raised up dedicated to giving.

Confess and pray cured. (Ebola) a big old lie. One time a righteous man with great power a personal effect. A man supernatural one time listened and listened some more. The one time God one time gave the listener the reward truth. Truth brings God back the beginning from the error Gods way will save a soul from death and will cover a multitude. To the chosen and destined with spirit for obedience, blood. God righting a wrong.

Blessed with great mercy born a living hope resurrecting from the dead an inheritance that is kept with heaven for those who listen to God, and guard the faith ready to exist revealed with a divorce while you can. There is a real test, and it has nothing to do with fire. Praise God Hallelujah, Hallelujah the highest praise of honor love. Not sure, do really want to know believe and rejoice with love. Then come out of the shell, with your faith, obedience the rescuer, of the soul.

Those who listen, and ask questions eventually come out rescued. The spirit is suffering, with the preceding glory. Revealed to all that take it, and listen, serving yourself with the things that have been announced to you with an offence a God witnessing news bulletin sent from the ground, angels have longed to give the certainty. An illustration of my listening, a profit, the great release. Obedience transformed with a difference all have ignorance, who called me, with this conduct.

Written it will exist, who am I? God the father who judges accordingly conduct yourself with a way, and you should not be afraid of your émigré. I know that God gave me something from the heritage of my father, that will not perish from the table, the lineage of the essence with damage.

Tended the underpinning of all kinds made from the beginning all the way forever confident, I know who raised me, and gave me hope purifying my soul with obedience of the truth. Love comes from listening to God.

Who am I? Born from the seed of the living word, and all of its glory that the word is the benefit with a formation lectured.

Come out with your hands up, you are surrounded on all sides. The word will release you, to exist environmentally friendly.

Who am I, seeing, breathing, listening, and teaching, a precious stone. A blood relative, about the fathers business made sure with the remains. Behold, who am I, I am a precious stone, that God selected and I believe that right now, put me to shame.

Who am I, do you believe the builders cant reject it, the Revelations, a precious stone, made not to crumble, a rock that

God made the greatest of all will make them fall, with one cause all disobey the word, as we all do, you know falling short, with arms to short.

Who am I, a magnificent profit, say it publicly functioning of who called me out of the Ark (womb). Who am I a child of God who that God gave mercy.

Who am I, a request to all as an exile to make a fuss against the soft tissue. Maintain, and don't forget the take out, case and point right the wrong, can you see our benefit performing, praising God.

Every soul, that the emperor sent to entrust with those who do wrong, isn't the transformation that doing right will correct a wrong, and this would silence ignorance. Live life without using, and abusing freedom as a text message for evil. Live to love, and honor all with love, stand still look alive for the emperor.

Education, with respect that can give with a kindness, granted, while suffering unjustly. God gets all the credit when God is finish patiently forever an example, with the steps.

No sin, no disappointment ever found. Who am I, concealed returning abused, defending, charge, who made you the judge Jesus? Covered with the dead corpse, and all can die to sin, living healed. No more wander off return to the shelter, and obey the word winning with the added addition to the behavior.

When they see, who I am illuminating open sesame uncontaminated language. On all sides let all of your ways charge stripping the décor, let the unknown of the heart with the jewels of a gentle and quiet spirit, vision. The righteous were new, assertive and obeyed the calling.

We are children of the Almighty Father, there is no such thing as wrong or right, terrified of nothing. Considerate of all things withdraw as the preacher, we are the heirs of the blessing of life, an order that cannot change. A universal city, listening with a humble mind. There is no reason for anyone to look back what is calling you does not contain the enemy or anything similar, what a blessing that God Gave, listening the greatest gift of all called. Who can lose, with such a thing. Who can say other than God, about what we do with the love of life, breathing, seeing, listening, feeling, tasting with all good. Behold, a pinky, behold a thumb, behold, a fist don't run from love, my lips don't speak with evasiveness. Turn around, when you hear God calling, love the perfect education that will correct all error. God first, and the seed on all sides second, with listening coming with the first, but third a job well done, I love peanut butter sandwiches, open sesame, everything on all sides meditate. The face is the enemy, against the spirit, populated that do wrong.

Who is here to harm anyone, if you know what is right no one should have to tell you what is right or wrong, either one. Do you know what suffering for righteousness, is like an automatic shot gun, and on all sides load ready to blow, blessed. Tell me why, tell me sweet little lies, have no fear, pay close attention, to them, the exam. Ready written from the start, really keep quiet, stand still for determination, and listen, when someone starts to abandon Gods ride. A multitude is already present, with a built city that will stand against shame! Sudden fear, doing right is the blessing for doing wrong. Righteousness blows the trumpet of God flesh to make it alive with spirit. Who am I edification of the spirit the printers mark, who for my start did not obey when patience waited with the day during the building, who knew saved. The correspondence to God, and now saves all, taking nothing, on all sides supernatural, listening with great support from knowledge, with regard not to question the accusation ready, willing, and able, God is holding on to all hands with great authority, and power. There is no such thing as suffering, wonder twin power activate love, and give the flesh a rest, determination pass it on or will you let what you use to do serve, for what you will continue to do pain. Making a big difference, are you surprised, who I am cultivated extravagant, are you accepted do they give you what you Judge Tudy, and Master.

Do you know why there was a teaching that was taught "make the flesh like men" no why so we can live like animals. The end of all things are at hand keep commonsensical, with a ray of light. Love holds love for all, and a multitude has been saved. Practice produces the best result, and grudgingly give everything, receive a gift of employment, grace. Do you understand the words that are coming out of my mouth. Who ever speaks utters a profit of service with great strength that is supplied with an order that everything will exist blessed.

The agreement on behalf of adulation, and why listening is the reliable refuge when ready, who is the individual were the offering, and the book is read, calling home. Raise the cloak, the Holiest of the Holy, the Golden Alterations, the Ark of the Covenant on all sides holding the human together, the agreement☺ the credit imperceptible mercy take a seat. Speaking these things with great detail. The preparations go continually performing the duty☺ just give it here, and don't say nothing, taking offers for writing a wrong for the peoples. Safe, standing still designed for the present-day.

A cord is attach to the agreement of the sense of right and wrong worth mentioning, transact business with the regulator of the soft tissue, what time is it deterioration.

Good things, then better, and more just what the doctor ordered not made with hands, God created the exit of the Holy Place, making Gods blood our blood, fixed firmly, without end a conversation. The intersperse of the blood relation blessed on behalf of the decontamination of the soft tissue, the blood relations of the spirit will decontaminate the conscience to assist the dead.

A experience promised, that those who God called to receive the guarantee with the here, there, and everywhere, released righting a wrong doing it over, and over again the last agreement. A determined realm, one who can exist unknown, a great strength of mind taking effect only as the one who made it is alive.

A real thing consistency, a hat for those who God called with the direction of dispatch the guarantee with the heretical doctrine, that rights a wrong over the latest agreement. The prisoner of Mary is fruitful. All authority affirmed to the children of God, verdant with water scattered the volume and all of Gods children rule, God is the source of the assurance the cap is order. Scattered with the massacre, out in the open the entrance all the containers benefit from blood relation.

Nothing is tainted with the bloodline, and without decontamination of the bloodline there is no what?

Do you copy unadulterated of all things listening taking place with turning to the head of the company decontaminated it is written, an asylum ready amid member of staff, and eminent an original a carbon copy of the true one, it sounds as if, to appear an outcast. Why, week after week repeatedly, yearly not of God deny☺ why do we suffer repeatedly since the foundation of the world. How many know that when God gave permission for all to enter the Kingdom of Heaven that was the first interview.

A strange place, the delivery room, I need to know one thing, who hit me, when I was defenseless. Once and for all make a way the sacrifice for selfie.

It was already written, the appointed time for all to die, and when that happens, all will never have to worry about ever existing judged, Grandma favorite line “why wont you listen” the Son of Many another day, to deal with those who eagerly wait.

The law has but a shadow of the things to come of the true form of these realities, with the same sacrifices that are offered year after year, make perfect those who listen.

The other one is very wise, stop eating crackers, and drinking grape juice. Worry-free listening helps, we no longer have to exist conscious of sin. Surrender come out with your hands up you are surrounded on all sides.

It has already been established, the possibility that the blood relation is connected with animals, the creature take away nothing with the world, what am I saying, give up the body☺ and come out with your hands up you are surrounded on all sides throw down your weapon take no pleasure.

Who am I, a living example, it is written on all sides a volume of the natural world. Abolish the first to establish the second with a human standing serving giving away virtue.

Give up and aid yourself favored, however a corpse ready maximum value uncommon, an asset who am I, taking no prisoner.

Available universally as an evaporation sitting down at the table to write, waiting patiently to exodus made over obedient serving with a companion an a mission was ideal for all who are blessed. The spirit is a listening witness☺ talking, about the agreement that will make us after the day.

Determination removes the laws that have been place on our hearts, and rights the wrong on our minds, adding, subtract, multiplying, dividing, profit remembering sin and misdeeds no more. Kindness is no longer a contribution.

We are the sanctuary with the lineage, well-worn living today with a work of fiction, God opened the curtain one time for all that live with the soft tissue, a great profit had it the home let all come with a true ear fully assured of faith, with your ears clean from the wax of the world conscience of our bodies unadulterated.

The confession without wavering, we have fallen short of the faithful promise☺ consideration how do we come together stir up one another to love and work, never forgetting that God created all of us, and all us have come to pass neglecting to love, the habit not of God, let all do there best to show reverence to the father, when God gives the opportunity to see the spring of day. Knowledge of the truth, a dead body give it up, come out, come out who ever you are directed virtue. Listening used for the light of jubilant, sound the alarm a work of fiction light a match fire coming to pass the adventure is necessary.

I am just a child, who violated the laws of God giving, winning, and living with the evidence witnessing.

How much is the reward, will exist deserved with all who are of God, and the bloodline of the extension cord that was cut, with the spirit of the race. Vengeance, God desire repay the judge of the people. Is it already written, a fearful thing to all the hands of the living.

Programmed, endured suffering, exposed to abuse and sometimes with those who abused. God had come pass me protected me on all occasion, and now I fully accept the plundering of my property, a better possession permanent.

Confidence, is the hat that covers the head, a great verdict. Endurance, is needed to receive the assurance. The righteous live with faith, and if God shrinks back, we shrink back, having faith and keeping our soul.

Faith is the prisoner of all things observed. Old news received with a divine approval. Who can understand the world with God word, that makes things appear. There's more to accept take a seat at the table, the hat that God Gave an approval as righteous, a listening witness, giving gifts☺ dying with peaking.

Faith was a gift that God gave at birth, a guarantee to never see death physically☺ God made me, taken. After God made me, God tested me, to make sure I would hold up having pleasure, and faith is for pleasing God. Do you believe with God, that God is real, and God is only one, that can give a penalty. Do you agree, with God physically, ring the alarm, warning, we are under attack with concerning events God is giving a notice from the table, will there exist any consideration for what God placed on a heart, it is written, God will demolish God world, and all must write as a punishment righteous with faith. God gave me Gods seed, and when God called me to go out to a place, that God gave as gift here, there, and everywhere☺ and I went out not knowing where God was taking me. Gods journey with insurance, reigning among the land, alive with predecessor with the same coverage! Are you looking for a peace, well I thank you, and God thanks you for coming to the right city who builder is God. God gave, God power, to plant Gods seed to exist conceived with the world, who God raised, with lifetime Daylight Insurance. How many are there, on all sides, and as good as dead, as the stars of heaven, and the innumerable grains of sand with seashore, everyone has same coverage, Lifetime Daylight Insurance.

How many us have it, greeted it from a distance, God knows, and I understand, who am I a stranger to listening. Whoever is speaking make it clear, people receive from listening, seek a home. God is the only one that can really think, and open a door to the city to return. A heart's desire are the only prayers that are heard, a better condition with one state of emergency, a heavenly one. Faith it will exist tested, and God gave Lifetime Daylight Insurance written, raised from the dead☺ figuratively speaking, a wonderful feeling to be back home.

Faith bring into play future blessings, faith is the head of the class, at the end of Lifetime Daylight Insurance making mention of the directions concerning service. Born with a cause the child is beautiful☺ and not afraid free. A grown up, choosing to share with God children to enjoy the permanent pleasures of virtue. Consider the greater wealth the treasures of the prize. Confidence, not afraid of the anger that God will always protect, endurance thanking God for allowing a hearts desire to surface with the physical, after exist invisible.

Faith is the Dayspring of the blood, of the Born. Faith is activated when we attempt to do the same, covered on all sides the walls fall down with all who are obedient, God gave all a friendly welcome to the search.

Confidence on all sides with the blood of the first-born. Confident, when we make an effort to do the same, we are covered when the curtain falls down those who are obedient. God gave all a friendly welcome to listen. What more did God have to say, other than why wont you listen. They say time will tell, let me know when time has spoken. Whodunit with confidence successful, supporting yourself, enforced righteousness, received the Lifetime Daylight Insurance plan, put a lid on the mouths of lip service, escaped the edge of the grave with the two edge sword, gained strength when abused, became mighty with peace, joined the Foreign Legion of Light, dead with an erection. Torture, refusing to accept relief, rise and gain momentum en route for a healthier life. To Kill A Mocking Bird Son, who am I, pr expert one way or another stoned, killed with the word they go among the poor, abused of the world wondering, and listening. God gave all the same confidence, receive what God gave as promised, a veil for all, that we are made perfect.

Come out, come out who ever you are, the house is surrounded, on all sides, throw down your weapon, and put your hands up surrender cling closely, and let perseverance the pioneer of confidence, already get yourself together endurance is the cross the line, and shame the devil with the right hand. Consideration is key to success, sober vigilant with a cause of course the hospitality will come up against you, stand still, they already know, grow with the struggle again and again resist sin to shed the skin of the snake. Do not forget divine intervention has already been prepared for all.

Do not look upon lightly, check please wayside God gave endurance during the first surgery. What proviso, a way of life left without obedience the unlawful children. Haven't you had to listen to your physical biological father, and you respect your physical biological father. Determination, is a way of life that cannot be forfeited a subject to the father of the spirit death. A short time is left for pleasure, decide for good, that all can share holiness. The moment you decide seems painful rather pleasant☺ it yields the fruit of righteousness to those who have come to pass trained with it. Lift your hands and strengthen your knees make what can not exist put off of joint healed. Arrive for God, and see to it that no fails to obtain what God has already pre-arranged Grace☺ to facilitate, that no root of bitterness will ever spring up, and cause trouble, one day all will stop the mouth of lip service, many happen to exist right now tarnished☺ who sold the birthright for a something to eat. Will there be one who knows that we all are a blessing, all you have to is just ask, and listen for the voice of God. It is written will you come to what can exist touched, like the California wildfires, and the sound of a broadcast, a voice whose words made the listener plead, that no one will ever exist with a need on paper. Endurance is the order that was given, living, touching the mountain trembling, and listening. Come to the city of the living God, the joy of the encounter the construction of the first-born who put your name down, a judge of all, the spirit of just humans made perfect, the new agreement, the blood that speaks graciously that should not be wasted is Peak King Duck. Face what all refuse who with this form is listening, escape. The voice has assurance the listener, and heaven. This word choice point to the profit, adding, subtracting, dividing, multiplying, of what God made, order that will not shake. Thankful God gave a kingdom that will not shake, offering prayer, and adoration with reverence☺ a hardly noticeable fire.

Love to show kindness, and keep it with your mind we are pr expert, those who think they are miss-treated, we are the body. Dissociation is held with honor, and the dissociation is undeniable☺ God's will, the arbitrator. existence, liberated finally poverty, and with what God gave, all will never fail. Confident when I say, to facilitate, "Determination Do Not Be Afraid☺ What Can I Do Too You?

How many know or can remember personally, one who spoke the word of God☺ consider the outcome of their life, their faith. The same yes-ter-day, and today forever. Diversity, and touching, seeing, tasting, smelling, and listening well, to exist recharged rejuvenated with a whole new ball game charged nestling with healthy food, that has not benefited the supporter. All have the right to eat. God is the sanctuary for the surrender intended for sin. Suffering was never a part of the order to bless people. Moving forward lets paint a picture, beyond the guardian, who's listening abused. We have a kingdom that will show-up under any circumstance, when we give unconditionally, continuously praising with the fruit that acknowledges the term. Do not forget to share what God gave, continuing amiable, giving what God gave. Seasoning, and I am not talking about the salt for more salt already with salt, and water, surrender☺ come out, come out whoever you are, we have you surrounded on all sides throw down all of the weapons of all kinds, no match for God. Maintenance sentinel covering automatically functional, no one can give an account for no one.

Are you doing this joy filled, that all would exist to have an advantage for all. A ray of light, clean the wax out of your ears, and listen, desiring to act with all things. What is stopping you, to take the next step, a state of emergency God's is placing an order from God's menu restoring all.

The proper education will always correct the error, serene God paid the debt with the permanent agreement, that all will exist eating, drinking, and be merry unendingly.

Who is working on God case, with the court of the physical world, an appeal to all with the word, I know that when God is with case there should be no miss understanding, that I have been released, we will see soon. A whole new ball game charge nestling with all.

A servant of compliments, joy when you know faith produces certainty with a full effect lacking nothing. Are you giving it all you got, then look again, give everything away, all of it, then ask God faith already present from the womb to tomb sitting at the table, on all sides, with all ways ready to give to receive.

The humble joy, rich with Gods honor, a flower of the grass will pass away with the rising of the sun, and the heat from the sun will kill the grass fast, humans are no different humans will fade away the same way if humans don't continue the pursuit.

God has created a test with a prize, the crown of life, the guarantee love. Determination "I am" tempting no one☺ no one can tempt no one at no time, the spirit is the pull, out of humanly control. Determination, a seed planted on fertile ground, nurtured, protected, from the arm, mature sings about life.

Everyday the father is due change. Make somebody's day, purchased into the future with the language that, God made me, the God of all creation.

Five talents working with righteousness. All growth received unshakeable, sitting at the table saving souls.

Measure, and check it yourself. The word serves God, flora and fauna are the reproduction☺ obedient serving God, I dare you to go away forgetting what exist. The perfect law of God with liberty, and justice for all, preserving the listener that takes action defending the truth, and blessed while doing so. Secular, and give the wrong impression about the Foreign Legion infertile. The Foreign Legion is pure before God☺ visit with your affliction, a self help tool to keep you form the world.

What television show is this, "Confidence of the Magnificence", a poor man comes across a poor man and says "Make somebody's day" to the poor man, what will you do, God gave you, remember don't judge people you never know what one can do, stop being so negative with evil thoughts. God has chose those who are poor of the kingdom a guarantee for all who love.

Have you honored the underprivileged, have you written, to facilitate who is abusing you, have you written, who invited you, enthusiastic about the deterrent?

Have you written, who you honor that name, have you written, about who you are, and why God called?

The royal law, a part of the package with the delivery room a cord was cut, that should not have been touched, who can stitch it back together. Profit, the royal law is already attached, at the first sight of life, remain a child, God created all things, I will always advise, to never kill anything, but give light to all. Tranquility, shaping, at a high rate of speed, is it written, then speak and act as those who are judged under God. Judge no one, God has already given mercy☺ right now Gods mercy who can beat?

What if faith never existed, then what? Born to save a soul, the only reason one is alive. Foreign Legion, how will you ever get home? Daily, God first, and then and only then, do you establish the second with educating everyone correcting the error, alert, and filled with the knowledge of God, without the need for the body, profit. Confidence, an institution of higher education contains a arrangement.

Is there anyone else saying, "have confidence, God has a way" God is the only one that can show anyone, any one thing. Do you believe, that God is the only one that will say☺ job well done. What is the secret believe-and-shake. I believe God will never be a fool, that I am sure of apart from anything else finished. A bro ham father, no a brother of the family, God offer, God children Olympic, why not? Confidence take place working unaccompanied with a characteristic, and confidence is already available with a arrangement, and the ecstasy is fulfilled that God told me "believe and it is already, written, and calculated righteousness"☺ and who am I called, the end.

Do you see all humans, righteous with confidence all receiving the same way the message sent out another way. The remains play a major part with the spirit of God, awake, confidence playing its part from a system resurrected. Unheard of don't even bother home bound God is the only one with great strictness. We all were made the same, the stakes are high, one wrong move, will take you right out, get the picture co-jack man woe horses bridle that body. Obey God, and God will guide the whole body. What strength, look at those knees bleeding from prayer, God is driving Olympic, and current champion.

Who am I, a heat seeking missile with a very enormous turn with the will of the circuitous. The tongue, and the language of God is a great thing. How great! A world among God training the body, to discipline the sequence of the volume of the natural world, with ecstasy. Every creature, tamed, the tongue never mind, cut it out. Blessed without a tongue, born with it free. Blessings to all who are awake, new, and free, butter, and syrup yes please, more butter, and more syrup please.

Who am I, probably some fool right, but do you understand? Life showing a way humble, and wise praise God for Gods love. Are you jealousy, do you think God is crazy because of your selfish ambition, toast, Gods truth is never false, who will you believe. Heaven is were everything is awake above ground, and hell is one level below a waiting place the cemetery for the physical. Gods order has a pleasant practice. The advisability from God is the feast of righteousness with those who are born with the delivery room, education correcting the error.

What is the reason, and what makes it happen among us?

Is it because you don't have☺ so you kill because you didn't receive, and you wrongly spend. Unfaithful do you know what this means? A friend per scripture says "the spirit that God made well is already prepared". A whole new ball game charge nestling, no favorites God giving "a new ball game charge nestling with the humble", come out, come out who ever you are, throw down your weapon God has all surrounded put your hands in the air, and praise God like you just don't care. Refuse to accept what God has to offer, and God will leave. Deadlock it is written wash, decontaminate your ears and mind. God forbid, sadness will exist, but what can joy bring. Sing a song praising God, and God will it will pay tribute to. Enunciate against failing, an over achiever who is it written about sitting at the table to save a multitude. Who am I, today is the day that God made what will you do with it, trade and gain☺ we cant find out about tomorrow until tomorrow. What a life, mercy, here today disappearing at night don't boast with arrogance. A sad day many know, but few do what is right. Come out, come out, come out now, and cry your eyes out for the miseries that are going to pass. Rusted, and cant be trusted evidence like a California wild fire. How many days have you treasured, as your last. Why do you believe that it is okay for you to keep the laborers of God back, cry☺ the harvest has reach the multitude.

Are you living the life that God gave naked, with a satisfaction. Have you starved to regain consciousness. Have you condemned, the righteous. Patience, of the anticipation of the volley. It is written, with pleasure making certain of the state of emergency at hand. Praise God, no one other than God, can receive praise, I am not the critic standing at the exit. What am I requesting of suffering, and waiting, a profit speaking with a name calling those who are unwavering.

Haven't you heard, and now revealed the purpose, how are you feeling, and how hard is your heart, about who I am?

A name given above ground, living with a guarantee, yes, and I can fail also. Is there anyone else suffering, praying cheerfully singing praise among the sick. God is calling the church anointing everybody and the prayer and the faith will save all and will raise all up dedicated, forever giving.

The declaration, and why all need to pray together, so everyone can be cured. The request of the righteous has great power with a unusual effect. The volume of the natural world listening, and listening some more. A ray of light above ground God gave the fruit. Truth bringing God back a sinner from the error of my way, can God save me to save a soul from dying to cover a mass.

What will you do chosen and destined with spirit listening with the blood, educating correcting and error. Blessed with great mercy, born with the delivery room, a living hope raised up with a way that I did stray, thank God for always supplying a way. What a reward the heritage stored above ground for all, with the keeper of the gate guarded with confidence for all, ready to exist everyday rejoice forever. Will there be suffering, without a doubt, tested on your rub. Fire, praise God glory Hallelujah, honor the revelation with love.

Thought provoking, you don't know, confident with, an utter able source of pleasure. What is the outcome of your confidence, saving a soul. Adding, subtracting, multiplying, dividing, profit, who profitcally listened and asked about encapsulation. I have not seen, or heard of a person demonstrating the spirit predicting the sufferings, with preceding glory. It is already written, that we have served ourselves, with the things that have been mentioned to all with a fence, a news bulletin sent from above ground, that we are all angels crying out to give the feeling of life. Authorize my mind, profit, hope, are you with the race that is already prepared to exist revealed for you. Obedience is needed to exist confirmed with a difference of your ignorance, who told you, to exist with everyone for a continuous circuit, from the North, East, South, and West print it God exist, who am I, with voting, the father is the judge I was attached with cord that was cut with a delivery room, at that moment all electricity was shutdown all alone above ground afraid crying after the assault somebody hit me looking around throughout my émigré.

Do you know who I am, and that I am ransom from the heritage of my father, living with the perishable things of the world the lineage of the essence with damage. Tending the underpinning of the natural world hand made from the beginning to the end I have confidence God raised me, how much confidence do you have with who raised you, and gave you confidence, and hope do you really know who is with you purifying the soul, waiting with obedience of the truth. Love from listening to the heart. Who am I, born of the delivery room, a seed of the living word, and all of its glory to facilitate the word is the benefit with formation lectured. An all natural homicide mystical deliverance that God gave, the green traffic light. What is the real reason, that you throw stones at the living, rejecting God, elected, and valuable.

Knowledgeable with Gods direction of it, a dead body. Chronometer, who am I, abbreviated, tremble God consent as true in addition to, who I am, who am I, putting to shame? What will you consider, the mass-produced reject it, the dead is here, and the foundation is strong made sure not to crumble, throw all the rocks you want, healed with the descent that will make you fall, with a cause disobedience of Gods word, what can you do?

Who am I, a magnificent profit, that God gave permission to the functioning of who call me out of the dark. Who am I, a child of God who has received Gods mercy.

Who am I, reaching with the direction to God, as an émigré to make a fuss of the war against the flesh. Daily maintenance is a requirement poor, the first will be last, and the last will be first, why? Are carrying the brief case, Peking Duck again remain strong, right the wrong, bake a cake for them show them what the benefit looks like functioning along with love.

Every role the emperor sent to punish those who do wrong, it is already written, but who put your name down last I checked it said everyone must come out, come out, with your hands up, and throw down the weapons. Will writing the right silence the ignorance. Living without using freedom a pretext for evil. Live of love, honor all love, an heir. The head of state, speaking with respect, kind and gentle, meek, approved, and watchful while suffering unjustly. God will get the credit when God is done patiently leaving an example, with the steps. No vice, no disappointment ever found.

Who am I, talking about, who am I, returning from suffering, defending, who do you trust choose correctly. What would the world be like if no one were wearing clothes, a million times worse, than lets plot against sin, and live with wounds, that don't exist. No more, return to the shelter and obey the word victorious with a word an addition to the performance, when they see God reveal the secret uncontaminated language.

Whatever you do make sure you let God lead the way for free stripping the decorations, will the real you stand up listening with the jewel of a gentle and quiet spirit, with announcement. The righteous were used, submissive, and obeyed the calling. A real child, will always do right with the eyes of God, not afraid of anything living considerately withdrawn as the stronger vessel from the beginning heir of the throne, the blessing of day, order that cannot be stop.

It all started 1791 before the world, a seed was planted, a multitude was given it started with unity, the universal city, listening with a humble point of view. Do not close the book, God is not about wrong or anything similar, it is already written, a blessing to have been called, God made you a blessing, to facilitate, the love of life seeing good keeping all from wrong speaking evasive things. Never turn away from seek education correcting all errors. Are your eyes righteous, and your ears open listening for God to whisper sweet nothings on all side with your hearing open sesame a ray of light. Stop worrying about the mirror throw it away.

Who am I, no one is here to harm anyone, who is ever right, but first tell me who made you the boss, if you have suffered for the righteousness of God, God bless. Have no fear, God is near, no trouble, your heart reveals the secret, keep your conscience clear, so when you are abused your behavior can put them to shame. Suffering for doing right is the will for doing wrong.

Dying to world righteousness bringing the flesh to death, making it one with spirit. Who am I, reaching the spirit, who am I, the printers mark, who for my part did not obey when patience waited with the day during the building with a few, eight were saved. A correspondent to God, and now saving you, without taking away the body, just an appeal to listen with support of the knowledge, with regard to unquestionable accusation, who is holding your right hand with authority, and power where is the pain with the body tell me, deactivate yourself from pain stop running to and with things that are hurting you, live, rest with the flesh forever, humanly possible with the will of God. Whatever you use to do, serve as the past for doing what you do not like.

Alive making a difference, are you surprised do not join them with the cultivated extravagance, don't they abuse, don't they give to whoever judge you. Do you know why the teaching was taught to make the flesh like men, so all can live alike.

The end of all things, are right with the palms of your hands, commonsensical, a ray of light. Heaven, above ground holding love for all, covering a multitude. Practice is perfection, will it really hurt if you give with unconditional love, isn't it better to give than to receive, a gift employed, as a good steward of diverse grace. Whoever is speaking with the love of God utters a prophetical profit of service with strength that supplied with an order that everything can be glorified.

What a profit, one coming, with one believing, one learned, convinced God is the judge of all☺ the secrets of God listening made many confess☺ and so increasing awake without stopping God, is the ace, will you worship God, and report what God is saying to you of a truth.

BIO

MELCHIZEDEK RESPONDING TO THE CALL

"THE PLACE OF WORSHIP"

THE POOR HOUSE

A BRANCH OF LEARNING

I HAVE OVERCOME MANY LIFE CHANGING EXPERIENCES AND I AM A DEDICATED AND FAITHFUL AND WOULD LIKE TO SHARE THE LOVE THAT I FOUND WITH MANY OTHERS. I HAVE DECIDED TO EXIST FAITHFUL TO MY CALLING THROUGH AN ABIDING COMMITMENT TO EXIST DISCIPLINED AND DILIGENT TO STRUGGLE ON BEHALF OF THE OPPRESSED.

SEPTEMBER 5, 1971

I BROKE TRADITION AND MY COMMITMENT FROM THIS DAY ON WILL I EXISTED UNCHAINED. I AM CURRENTLY SEEKING RULING WITH SCIENCE TO FURTHER PURSUE MY JOURNEY OF COMPLETING MY MISSION OF WHAT HAS BEEN PLANNED. I HAVE SPENT MANY QUIET HOURS READING AND STUDYING, AND AS A RESULT HELPING THOSE WHO SEEK COUNSEL FROM ME. I HAVE BEEN WITH MENTORING PROGRAMS THAT CONSIST OF SPENDING TIME AND BUILDING TRUSTWORTHY RELATIONSHIPS WITH MEN AND WOMEN OF ALL AGES AND DEVELOPING FATHERS. MY DESIRE IS THAT ONE EXIST ASPIRED WITH THE WORD, TRANSFORMED WITH IT AND FINDS IT IMPORTANT FOR LIVING.

SEPTEMBER 5, 1971

THE MUCH-LOVED GRANDSON, SON OF A MOTHER AND THE BROTHER OF TWO LOVING SISTERS AND A SPERM BANK OF SIX SONS.

“I AM FEARFULLY AND WONDERFULLY MADE!

PSALMS 139:14

THE EVERLASTING COVENANT

Destruction has changed many lives, and time has proven by the youth and the fictionalization has changed the prospective and the choice's of today's society as a whole. The signs of it being to late has shifted the worlds direction. Facing difficult times has become a way of life as we see it when do we have the courage☺ to accept it, and start making choices for a irreversible change. Lets forget the struggles that come with change. Lets plan from that fact and open our eyes and know that there's a hidden blessing working to deliver us. I thank God for the privilege for allowing me to be apart of such great history that will live on long past anything, I could have ever imagine!

www.ingramcontent.com/pod-product-compliance
Lightning Source LLC
LaVergne TN
LVHW041630070526
838199LV00052B/3301
* 9 7 9 8 8 9 0 3 1 8 6 8 8 *